This book belong

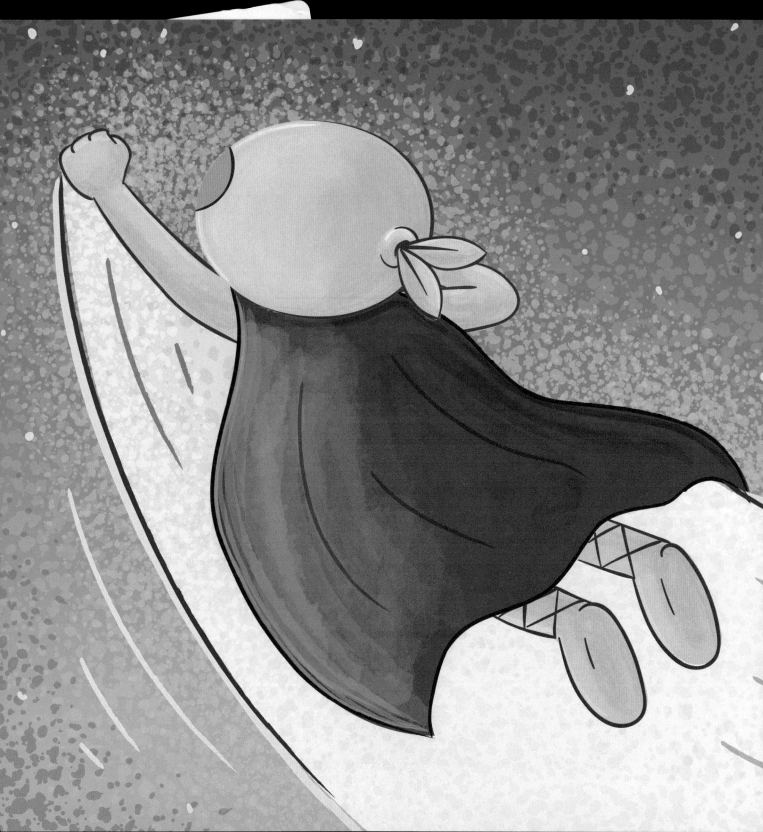

Paperback ISBN: 978-1-63731-708-2
Hardcover ISBN: 978-1-63731-710-5
eBook ISBN: 978-1-63731-709-9

Printed and bound in the USA.
NinjaLifeHacks.tv

Ninja Life Hacks®
by Mary Nhin

Neurodivergent Ninja

A Children's Book About the Gifts of Neurodiversity

Ninja Life Hacks®
by Mary Nhin

At home and at school, it can be hard for me to adapt to change.

Stay focused on an activity that I like for long periods of time.

Think outside-the-box which can lead to creative and new solutions to challenges.

Excel in music, art, technology, and science.

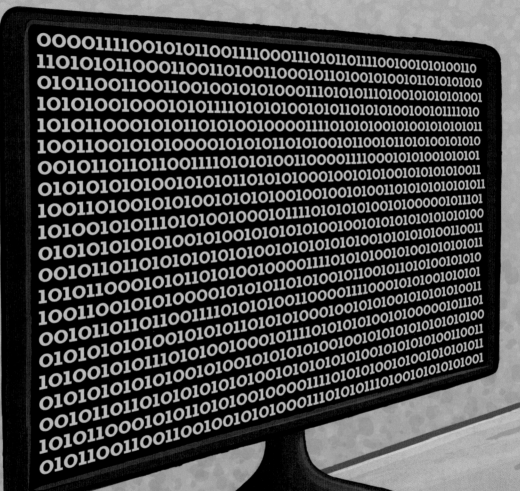

The best ways to bring about my gifts of neurodiversity is to practice a strategy I call the G.I.F.T. which stands for:

Get space if I'm overstimulated

Include visual charts and reminders

Find my mindful breath

Try tools to reduce distractions

I like to **include** visual charts and reminders in my daily routine so I can see clear paths.

G. I. F. T.

Get space if I'm overstimulated

Include visual charts and reminders

Find my mindful breath

Try tools to reduce distractions

Check out the Neurodivergent Ninja lesson plans that contain fun activities to support the social, emotional lesson in this story at ninjalifehacks.tv!

I love to hear from my readers.
Write to me at info@ninjalifehacks.tv or send me mail at:

Mary Nhin
6608 N Western Avenue #1166
Oklahoma City, OK 73116

Made in United States
Orlando, FL
23 February 2024

44045301R00022